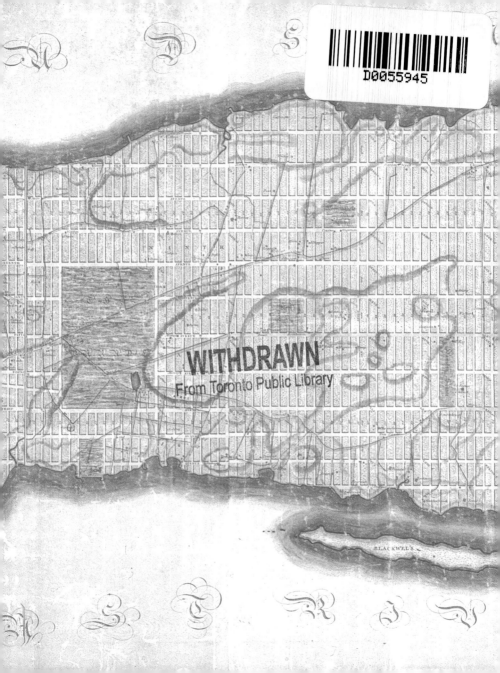

BLACKWEL'S

NEW YORK LANDMARKS

A COLLECTION OF ARCHITECTURAL
AND HISTORICAL DETAILS

Charles J. Ziga,
Annie Lise Roberts & Jeanne-Marie Hudson

UNIVERSE

*"Give me your tired, your poor,
Your huddled masses yearning to breathe free,
The wretched refuse of your teeming shore.
Send these, the homeless, tempest-tost to me,
I lift my lamp beside the golden door!"*

FROM "The New Colossus"
Emma Lazarus, 1883

NEW YORK LANDMARKS

INTRODUCTION

When the early explorers—Verrazano, Gómez, Hudson—sailed into New York Bay in the 16th and 17th centuries, they found neither the gold nor the spices that they sought, but they saw promise. By the mid-1600s, the Dutch had begun to colonize Manhattan (then New Amsterdam), having "purchased" the land from American Indians for about $65. Lured by the potential of its strategic trade location, fertile land, and religious freedom, a variety of Europeans began arriving in New York, and settlements throughout what would become the five boroughs began emerging.

By the late 17th century, the Dutch had lost control of New York to the British, but traces of their influence in early New York remain. Having always feared a British invasion, then-governor Peter Stuyvestant had a barricade built along the northern boundary of the New Amsterdam settlement (now lower Manhattan); the wall was dismantled by the British in 1699, but the street that replaced it was and still is known as Wall Street, historically—and presently—the seat of the city's influential financial industry. In 1789, George Washington was inaugurated as the nation's first president at New York's first City Hall (now Federal Hall), on Wall Street, and thus New York was briefly our nation's first capital city; Trinity Church at Wall and Broad Streets (the third on this site) also bears testimony to the area's long history, revealing gravestones dating back to 1681.

Roots had been planted and New York began to fulfill its promise. By the early 1800s the city was an economic powerhouse, and the construction of the Erie Canal in 1825 solidified the importance of New York's Atlantic waterways in opening up the country's interior. Immigration boomed and the city expanded and benefited from the diverse influx of residents. Arriving at Ellis Island, the country's busiest immigrant-receiving station, newcomers caught sight of the Statue of Liberty, a goodwill gift from the French that seemed to epitomize the greatness of the nation's most significant city. Entrepreneurs with wealthy benefactors, and visionary leaders and civil servants transformed New York into an enviable urban center; parks sprung up, bridges spanned, museums opened, theaters beckoned, and skyscrapers attempted to outdo one another in height and ingenuity. By the turn of the 20th century, New York's wealth and prosperity were unrivaled.

Today, New York is a thriving heterogeneous city whose buildings and spaces bear witness to its remarkable foundations. Be it the ornate architecture of a centuries-old church, the private-turned-public collection of a philanthropic New York–made millionaire, the progressive design and construction of the city's first steel buildings, or the green spaces created as sports field or sanctuary, New York City's landmarks are as diverse as its population. The physical evolution of New York City is inextricably bound to its cultural evolution, a true melting pot of traditions, ideals, and resourcefulness all rolled up into one juicy Big Apple.

"No other American city is so intensely American as New York."

—ANTHONY TROLLOPE
English novelist

CITY HALL

New York's architectural treasure

City Hall Park, between Broadway and Park Row

City Hall, completed in 1812, is home to the Mayor's office and City Council Chambers and is the oldest and longest serving City Hall in the United States. It is New York's welcoming center for important dignitaries, returning soldiers, celebrities, and athletes. This elegant scaled-down palace combines the *Georgian-Federal* style with *French Renaissance* details. The building is situated in City Hall Park, the town green of the city. Since colonial times, the park has been the site of parades, protests, riots, and celebrations.

Joseph F. Mangin and **John McComb**, *Architects*. Awarded the commission by their competition-winning design. McComb is attributed with the *Georgian*-style interior and Mangin, a French émigré, with the elegant *French Renaissance* details and graceful ornamentation of the exterior.

The symmetrical two-story building features a one-story central portico and projecting wings. The facade's rows of arched windows are decorated with Corinthian pilasters to each side and swags above. The building was originally finished in white marble with the base and north facade of New Jersey brownstone. Upon its completion in the early 1800s, City Hall was at the northern edge of New York City, and therefore the northern side was clad in brownstone in order to save money. The clock in the cupola was added in 1831 and was the first illuminated clock in New York City. A figure of Justice, designed by John Dixey, crowns the cupola.

The interior is classic *Georgian*. At the central rotunda (inset) is a sweeping pair of self-supporting marble stairs. On the second floor of the rotunda, 10 Corinthian columns support a coffered dome with a glass oculus.

Fire and decay prompted major renovations over the decades, including replacing the crumbling exterior with Alabama limestone in 1956—all four sides now matching for the first time in history. Currently, structural and electrical improvements—with a price tag of nearly $100 million— are underway, scheduled for completion in time for the building's 200th anniversary in 2012.

National Historic Landmark 1960. N.Y.C. Landmark February 1, 1966.
Interior Landmark January 17, 1976.

SCHERMERHORN ROW

Street of ships

Fulton Street, at the South Street Seaport

Built between 1811 and 1812, in the *Georgian-Federal* tradition of architecture, Schermerhorn Row was one of the earliest commercial developments in New York City. When the area was a major shipping center, its 12 buildings housed chandleries (selling provisions for ships), sail lofts, rope lofts, and naval store warehouses.

Peter Schermerhorn, *Merchant and Ship Owner.* Constructed these buildings for lease to sailing merchants. Schermerhorn operated his own prosperous ship chandlery from 243 Water Street.

The four-story row houses—derived from 18th-century English counting halls—on Fulton Street, Front Street, and South Street were built on land-filled water lots (land between extremes of high and low tides). Red Flemish bond brickwork, plain stone lintels, arched entrances of brownstone, tall brick chimneys, and steep *Georgian* hip roofs of slate are the buildings' original features. The area became a busy commercial district in 1816, when the Brooklyn Ferry put a landing at Schermerhorn's wharf. Soon after, the Fulton Market opened across the street. In the late 1800s, dormers and *Greek Revival*–style cast-iron storefronts were added to the building to serve ships' passengers. In 1868, the building on the corner of South and Fulton Streets was converted into a hotel. The fifth story and the mansard roof with dormers were added for additional rooms.

In 1968, Schermerhorn Row was protected by the New York City Landmarks Commission and became an integral part of the South Street Seaport Historical District. It was restored in 1983 by **Jan Hird Pokorny** and **Cabrera & Barricklo**, *Architects.*

N.Y.C. Landmark October 29, 1968.

"*You will find that New York possesses the advantage of a capacious and excellent roadstead, a vast harbour, an unusually extensive natural basin, with two outlets to the sea, and a river that in itself, might contain all the shipping of the earth.*"

—JAMES FENIMORE COOPER
American novelist and essayist

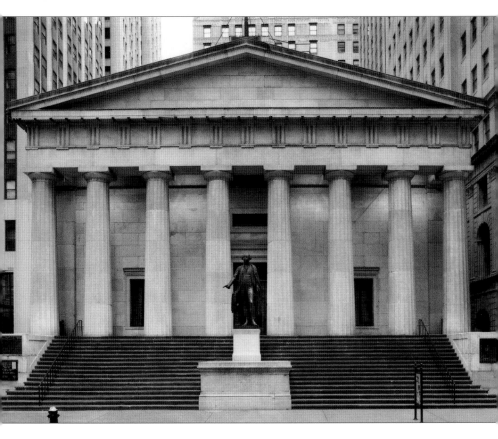

"*No people can be bound to acknowledge and adore the Invisible Hand which conducts the affairs of men more than those of the United States.*"

—GEORGE WASHINGTON
First Inaugural Address
Thursday, April 30, 1789

FEDERAL HALL NATIONAL MEMORIAL

Site of the first capitol of the United States

26 Wall Street

Federal Hall National Memorial is situated on one of New York's most historic sites. Here once stood New York City's first City Hall (later called Federal Hall) where the first U.S. Congress met and where George Washington took his oath as the first U.S. president in 1789. In 1812, the original building was demolished and sold as salvage for $425. The current building, constructed between 1834 and 1842, was originally a U.S. Custom House. It later became a U.S. Sub-Treasury. Today, it serves as a museum for American and New York history. Just four blocks from Ground Zero, the museum underwent a $16 million renovation in 2005–2006 to repair cracks in its foundation aggravated by the 9/11 collapse of the Twin Towers.

Ithiel Town and **Alexander Jackson Davis**, *Architects.* Awarded the commission based on their *Greek Revival* design.

Samuel Thompson, *Construction Architect.* **John Frazee**, *Interior Architect.*

The ideals of Greek democracy and Roman republicanism that influenced the Founding Fathers were reflected in their choice of classical architecture for public buildings. This classic Greek temple rests on a high plinth with a steep flight of steps. A portico with 32-foot-high Doric columns supports a simple pediment without ornamentation.

The interior rotunda (inset) is dominated by a paneled dome (not a typical Greek form) that is 60 feet in diameter and is supported by 16 two-story-high Corinthian columns. The rich, ornate Roman interior contrasts with the simple Greek exterior.

The statue of *George Washington* is by J. Q. A. Ward, 1883.

National Historic Landmark 1939. N.Y.C. Landmark December 21, 1965.
Interior Landmark May 27, 1975.

TRINITY CHURCH AND CHURCHYARD

A green oasis amid the concrete

Broadway at Wall Street

Completed in 1846, after seven years of construction, Trinity Church served the first Episcopalian parish in New York City and was the tallest building in the area until the late 1860s.

Richard Upjohn, *Architect.* English-American. Founder of the American Institute of Architects and its first president, 1857–76.

Richard Morris Hunt, *Architect.* Designed the six sculptured bronze doors illustrating biblical scenes and the history of Trinity Church. The bas-relief detail (inset) represents Revelation VI, verses 15, 16, and 17. Like Upjohn, Hunt was a founder of the American Institute of Architects.

The *Gothic Revival* church, 79 feet wide and 166 feet long, is built of New Jersey brownstone and has flying buttresses, stained-glass windows, Gothic tracery, and medieval sculptures. Located at the head of Wall Street, the central tower with octagonal spire measures 280 ½ feet tall. Its bells were imported from London in 1797 and are the oldest in New York. Trinity Church is the third church to be built on the site. King William III of England gave the land to the church in 1697, and the original church, completed a year later, was burned in the Great Fire of 1776. The second church was demolished in 1839 after structural failure.

Trinity Churchyard, established even before the first church (the oldest grave-stone dates from 1681), includes graves and memorials of historic New Yorkers such as Francis Lewis (signer of the Declaration of Independence), Alexander Hamilton (Secretary of the U. S. Treasury), William Bradford (founder of the city's first newspaper, the *Gazette*), and Robert Fulton (inventor). It remains one of the last green sites in the Financial District.

National Historic Landmark 1976. N.Y.C. Landmark August 16, 1966.

"*When Charles first saw our child Mary, he said all the proper things for a new father. He looked upon the poor little red thing and blurted, 'She's more beautiful than the Brooklyn Bridge.'*"

—HELEN HAYES
American actress

BROOKLYN BRIDGE

World's first steel-wire suspension bridge

Manhattan (City Hall Park) to Brooklyn
(Cadman Plaza)

On May 24, 1883, after 13 years of construction, the Brooklyn Bridge became the first bridge to span the East River, uniting the boroughs of Brooklyn and Manhattan. The bridge was constructed at a cost of over $15 million.

John A. Roebling, *Engineer.* An immigrant from Prussia and original designer of the bridge. While directing the bridge's surveying, he was injured in an accident and died before construction began.

Colonel Washington A. Roebling, *Chief Construction Engineer.* After suffering an injury while inspecting work inside one of the caissons, Roebling became an invalid and oversaw the remaining construction from the window of his Brooklyn Heights home, with the help of his engineer-trained wife.

With its two *Gothic* towers (inset) rising 276 feet, the bridge was the second highest structure in New York in 1883. Only the spire of Trinity Church was taller. One of Roebling's greatest innovations was the first-ever use of steel (for its superior strength) rather than iron wires for the bridge's four main cables. Each cable, 15 ¾ inches in diameter, contains 5,434 wires, and is 3,515 feet long. The bridge stretches 5,989 feet overall, with a center span of 1,595 feet between its two towers, and is 85 feet wide. Today, more than 145,000 vehicles and steady pedestrian traffic cross the bridge daily.

One week after its grand opening, 12 pedestrians were trampled to death on the bridge's promenade when the crowd panicked, thinking the bridge was collapsing.

In 2006, workers conducting a routine inspection discovered a Cold War–era supply chamber inside the Manhattan-side foundation, stocked with decades-old food and supplies needed to survive a nuclear attack on New York City.

National Historic Landmark 1964. N.Y.C. Landmark August 24, 1967.

SAINT PATRICK'S CATHEDRAL

Dedicated to the patron saint of Ireland

Fifth Avenue, between 50th and 51st Streets

Saint Patrick's is the largest Roman Catholic church in the U.S. and the seat of the Archdiocese of New York. The cathedral took 21 years to build: four times longer than planned and at twice the estimated cost. Cardinal John McCloskey formally blessed and opened the cathedral on May 25, 1879. The spires were completed nine years later, and the Lady Chapel was added in 1906.

Archbishop John Hughes, *First Catholic Archbishop of New York.* Irish immigrant. Announced his plan for Saint Patrick's as a church "worthy of God…and an honor to this great city." Construction began in 1858.

James Renwick Jr., *Architect.* Renwick also designed the original Smithsonian Institution building, "the Castle," in Washington, D.C.

Ridiculed as "Hughes' Folly" for its ambitious scope and its remote location on the city's outskirts, the site of the cathedral was formerly home to a Jesuit school for young men, a Trappist community and its orphanage, and a future cemetery. Upon completion, the spires of Saint Patrick's dominated the surrounding skyline until the 1930s. Today, the cathedral is dwarfed by the glass and steel skyscrapers of midtown Manhattan.

The *French Gothic* cathedral, 174 feet wide and 332 feet long, is the eleventh-largest church in the world. Constructed of white marble, it is in the shape of a Latin cross with traditional east-west orientation. Above the central entrance is a circular rose window, 26 feet in diameter, flanked by foliated tracery spires 330 feet high. The north tower holds the cathedral's chimes of 19 bells. Three sets of bronze doors adorned with statues of the saints of New York, designed by Charles Maginnis and John Angel in 1949, comprise the cathedral's formal entrances. The bas-relief detail from the central doors (inset) represents Elizabeth Ann Seton, the first American-born saint.

The nave (central seating area) is 108 feet high and 48 feet wide. Forming the cathedral's focal point is the sanctuary, with its 57-foot-high bronze baldachin.

National Historic Landmark 1976. N.Y.C. Landmark October 19, 1966.

"*The Dakota was a daring building and a daring venture. Although its situation seemed enviable—the peace and quiet, the unobstructed light, the country air, the boundless vista—many New Yorkers thought the view to a vast greensward was a lonely prospect.*"

—ELIZABETH HAWES
American author

DAKOTA APARTMENTS

It might as well be in the Dakota Territory

72nd Street and Central Park West

The city's first luxury apartment house was named for the remote northwestern Indian territory because it was located so far from the city's center. At the time of its completion in 1884, the building was surrounded by vacant land and squatters' shacks. Early Dakota residents had views of Central Park (still incomplete), Long Island Sound, the undeveloped hills of Brooklyn, and the Hudson River.

Edward S. Clark, *Singer Sewing Machine Heir, Developer.* He turned public mockery of his building's location to good account in both name and decoration. Western ornamentations of arrowheads, sheaves of wheat, and an Indian head relief (inset) are incorporated into the design.

Henry J. Hardenbergh, *Architect.* Also designed the Plaza Hotel.

Reminiscent of a fortress-like château, the eight-story yellow brick mass is articulated by brownstone and terra-cotta gables, bay windows, recessed and projecting balconies, cornices, trim, and ornamentation. The steeply pitched slate and copper roof is adorned with chimneys, dormers, and pediments. Surrounding the *German-Renaissance* building is a stylized "moat" with sea monsters and masks of Zeus.

The main entrance, a two-story arched gateway on 72nd Street, leads into an inner courtyard with two fountains. At each of the courtyard's four corners is an entrance and elevator. There were originally 65 apartments on nine floors, each with 4 to 20 rooms (a typical living room measures 25 ft. x 40 ft.) with 12- to 15-foot ceilings and wood-burning fireplaces. Interiors finished in mahogany and oak boast marble mantels and brass fixtures. Walls 2 feet thick and 18-inch-thick floors make this one of the city's quietest buildings.

Famous tenants of the Dakota have included: Boris Karloff, Lauren Bacall, Leonard Bernstein, Judy Garland, John Lennon, and Yoko Ono.

National Historic Landmark 1976. N.Y.C. Landmark February 11, 1969.

STATUE OF LIBERTY

Liberty enlightening the world

Liberty Island (Bedloe's Island),
New York Harbor

France presented the statue on July 4, 1885, as a gift recognizing the friendship established between the two nations during the American Revolution. It took 10 years to build at a cost of $400,000. Lady Liberty arrived on Bedloe's Island (now Liberty Island) on October 28, 1886, in 350 individual pieces packed in 214 crates and ready for assembly.

Édouard-René Lefebvre de Laboulaye, *French Historian.* Paris. Credited with the idea of a statue symbolizing the union of France and the United States in the quest for liberty and freedom.

Frédéric-Auguste Bartholdi, *Sculptor.* Paris. The image was modeled after his mother and Delacroix's painting *Liberty Leading the People to the Barricades.*

Alexandre-Gustave Eiffel, *Engineer.* Paris. Engineered the statue's skeletal frame of iron and steel. He also designed the Eiffel Tower.

Richard Morris Hunt, *Architect.* Designed the statue's 151-foot-high pedestal of Stony Creek granite and concrete.

The statue, which stands 305 feet tall (with pedestal), is made of 300 copper sheets molded and riveted to and supported by the steel and iron framework. The length of the upraised arm with torch is 45 feet. Copper oxidizing gives the statue its green color (patina). One hundred fifty-four steps lead from the pedestal to the head. Though the torch has been closed to public access since 1916, the crown is open on a limited basis.

Broken shackles at Liberty's feet signify escape from tyranny; the 21-foot-tall torch symbolizes truth and justice illuminating the world; the spikes of her crown denote the seven seas and seven continents; and the tablet (inset) bears the date of the Declaration of Independence: July 4, 1776. After renovation by *architects* **Richard S. Hayden** and **Thierry W. Despont** (1984–86), she was rededicated on October 28, 1986, for her 100th birthday.

National Historic Landmark 1924. N.Y.C. Landmark September 14, 1976.

"If [Central Park] marks the geographical center of this densely packed island [Manhattan], it also marks a certain emotional core. This, after all, is where generations of New Yorkers have walked their dogs, pushed baby carriages, biked and skated, listened to music, thought deep thoughts and even married. For many, it was their first and last backyard."

—THE NEW YORK TIMES

CENTRAL PARK

New York's emerald treasure

59th Street to 110th Street, Fifth Avenue
to Eighth Avenue

With urging from merchants and landowners seeking outdoor space for the enjoyment of all residents, the city acquired more than 700 acres of land to be developed in the tradition of Europe's public gardens. Central Park, the first planned park in the United States, is one of New York's finest treasures, and since 1857 has continued to evolve to meet the changing needs of an urban society while retaining its designers' original intent.

William Cullen Bryant, *Editor of the* N.Y. Evening Post, and **Andrew Jackson Downing,** *Landscape Architect and Publisher of the* Horticulturist, were instrumental in gathering support for a large public park in New York City.

Frederick Law Olmsted, *Engineer and Landscape Architect,* and **Calvert Vaux,** *Architect.* Won the competition and the $2,000 award with their **Greensward Plan**. Their design integrated architecture with landscaping to accommodate the uneven topography.

The 843-acre park, 2 ½ miles long and ½ mile wide, is located in the heart of Manhattan Island. The park's southern half is more pastoral, with an open landscape, and its northern half is more rugged and wooded. Foot paths, bridal paths, curved carriage drives (to discourage carriage racing), and four sunken transverse roads provide for pedestrian and motor traffic. The 36 unique and original arched bridges that grace the park were all designed by Calvert Vaux. During construction, over a half million trees (632 species), vines (815 varieties), shrubs, and flowers were planted; 10 million cartloads of earth were moved.

The park's major points of interest are the Bethesda Fountain and Terrace (inset), Belvedere Castle, the Mall, Delacorte Theater, Strawberry Fields, Wollman Memorial Rink, the Conservatory Garden, and the Zoo.

National Historic Landmark 1963. N.Y.C. Scenic Landmark April 16, 1974.

CARNEGIE HALL

How do you get to Carnegie Hall? — Practice, practice, practice.

57th Street and Seventh Avenue

Carnegie Hall (formerly Music Hall) opened on May 5, 1891, with the American premiere of Peter Ilyich Tchaikovsky conducting his *Marche Solennelle*. Since then, it has become a world-renowned concert hall, as famous for its near perfect acoustics as for its extravagant architecture.

Andrew Carnegie, *Steel Magnate, Philanthropist.* A Scottish immigrant, he donated $2 million to build the concert hall at the urging of **Walter Damrosch,** Conductor of the Oratorio Society of New York and the New York Symphony Society.

William Burnet Tuthill, *Architect.* His research of European concert halls and the technology available 100 years ago resulted in the outstanding acoustics of Carnegie Hall.

The *Italian-Renaissance* exterior is of pale brown Roman brick with Roman arches, pilasters, and terra-cotta ornamentation (inset). Built entirely of masonry without a steel frame, it is one of the last of its kind in New York City, although 20th-century additions include steel framework. The original mansard roof was replaced by a sixth floor of studios, but the tower was retained. Carnegie Hall is an early example of a mixed-use building with offices, studios, shops, a theater, a recital hall, and a concert hall.

The famous acoustics are attributed to the soft curved planes of the balconies and the elliptical ceiling, which allows sound to be diffused throughout the 2,804-seat auditorium. The velvet drapery adorning the hall helps to absorb both reverberation and echoes.

The hall has been host to the world's greatest conductors, musicians, and performers including Arturo Toscanini, Leonard Bernstein, Ella Fitzgerald, Charlie Parker, the Rolling Stones, and the Beatles. In addition, it has served as a lecture hall for such notables as Martin Luther King Jr., Winston Churchill, Eleanor Roosevelt, and Mark Twain. In 1959, Isaac Stern, violinist, rallied support to save Carnegie Hall from demolition; in 1986 he played a central role in its restoration.

National Historic Landmark 1962. N.Y.C. Landmark June 20, 1967.

"And New York is the most beautiful city in the world? It is not far from it. No urban night is like the night there . . . Squares after squares of flame, set up and cut into the aether. Here is our poetry, for we have pulled down the stars to our will."

—EZRA POUND
American expatriate poet

WASHINGTON MEMORIAL ARCH

*Exitus acta probat
(The end justifies the deed)*

Washington Square North at Fifth Avenue

In 1889, a temporary wood and stucco arch was built to commemorate the centennial anniversary of the inauguration of George Washington as the first president of the United States. Building began on the current memorial arch in 1892, and it was dedicated on April 30, 1895.

William Rhinelander Stewart. Credited with the arch's concept and fund raising, $2,765 from the Washington Square residents.

Stanford White, of McKim, Mead & White, *Architect.* Designed both the wood and stucco arch and the marble arch modeled after the Arc de Triomphe in Paris.

Rising at the foot of Fifth Avenue, the *Beaux-Arts*-style white marble triumphal arch (77 ft. H x 30 ft. W x 10 ft. D) dominates the northern entrance to Washington Square Park. Two winged figures of Victory in relief are carved above the 47-foot-high arch. Emblems of war and peace adorn the columns, and a sculpted American Eagle, large decorative stars, and W's decorate the frieze. The west-pier sculpture by Alexander Stirling Calder (father of mobile-maker Alexander Calder) is *Washington in Peace* with *Justice* and *Wisdom* (inset). The inscribed Latin (*Exitus acta probat*) in the book behind Washington means "The end justifies the deed." On the east pier can be found *Washington in War* with *Fame* and *Valor*, by Herman A. MacNeil.

An icon of Manhattan's once-bohemian Greenwich Village, in 2003 the arch underwent a 14-month, $2.7 million restoration to reverse the effects of a century of pollution and neglect. On April 30, 2004, city officials rededicated the arch, whose facelift included a new roof, repairs to the Washington statues and the underside rosettes, and new lighting. The arch project is the first in the city's $16 million commitment to refurbish Washington Square Park (built 1827) to its former splendor.

N.Y.C. Historic District April 29, 1969.

IMMIGRANT RECEIVING STATION

First steps in a new land

Ellis Island, New York Harbor

The original Ellis Island Immigrant Receiving Station opened its doors to the first immigrant, Annie Moore of Cork, Ireland, in 1892. Five years later, it was destroyed by fire. The current building, in the *French Renaissance* style, cost $1.5 million. On December 17, 1900, its first day of operations, 2,251 immigrants were processed. Its peak year was 1907, when 1.2 million immigrants came through Ellis Island. The building remained the nation's primary immigration reception depot until 1924. Only 2 percent of the 12 million immigrants who passed through its doors were sent back to their countries of origin. The station closed as an immigration center in 1954, but has since served as a Coast Guard Station and an enemy-alien detention center.

William A. Boring and **Edward L. Tilton,** *Architects.*

The Immigrant Receiving Station is constructed of heavily rusticated limestone and red brick with limestone ornamentation. Between the three colossal arches of the entry are two limestone American Eagle statues (inset). Rising from the four corners of the central pavilion are four 134-foot-high copper-capped towers. Inside, on the second floor, is the building's grandest room, Registry Hall. Its 50-foot vaulted ceiling is adorned with interlocking terra-cotta tiles. Other buildings in this complex include the hospital, powerhouse, dormitories, and dining hall. The island itself grew from a sandbar to its current 27-acre size using earth excavated for construction of the New York City subway system.

In 1984, the building was closed for a $160 million renovation and restoration under the direction of **Beyer Blinder & Belle / Notter Finegold & Alexander**. It was reopened as a National Museum in September 1990. In the spring of 2010, restoration to the Main Building and repair of the seawall commenced, limiting visitor access to portions of the Wall of Honor until spring 2012.

National Historic Monument 1965. National Historic District 1993.

"To Europe she [New York City] was America, to America she was the gateway of the earth. But to tell the story of New York would be to write a social history of the world."

—H. G. WELLS
English novelist and historian

FLATIRON BUILDING

Twenty-three skidoo

175 Fifth Avenue at 23rd Street

The Flatiron Building (originally the Fuller Building after its developer) derives its popular name from its triangular shape created by the intersection of Broadway and Fifth Avenue at 23rd Street. It was one of the city's tallest buildings when it was completed in 1902, marking the beginnings of the skyscraper era in New York City.

Daniel H. Burnham of D. H. Burnham & Co., Chicago. *Architect.* Burnham also designed one of the earliest skyscrapers, the Monadnock Building, in Chicago, 1891.

Covering the entire lot, the 22-story, 285-foot-high building extends in an unbroken mass without any setbacks. The steel framework is clad with rusticated limestone and molded terra-cotta in the *Beaux-Arts* style. The vertical composition is the classic tripart, based on the divisions of a column (base, shaft, and capital top). The base (first four floors) is heavily rusticated, giving the building a solid anchor. The ornate capital, with two-story arches and an enormous cornice, provides a visual stop to the otherwise continuous 12-story shaft. Viewed from uptown on Fifth Avenue, the Flatiron Building has been compared to the bow of a ship. Its rounded apex at 23rd Street is only six feet across.

In the early 1900s, strong down drafts from the building created a spectacle of young ladies' long skirts being lifted, exposing their ankles. Reputedly, their admirers were cleared away with shouts of "Twenty-three skidoo" from the policemen directing traffic.

Currently a functioning office building, a majority stake in the property was purchased in 2009 by an Italian real estate investment firm intending to convert the iconic building into a luxury hotel, although the renovation cannot take place until all current leases expire.

National Historic Landmark 1989. N.Y.C. Landmark September 20, 1966.

MACY★S

The world's largest store

34th Street from Broadway to Seventh Avenue

From its modest beginnings as a "fancy dry goods" store, Macy's flagship location in Herald Square boasts more than one million square feet of retail space and 300 selling departments. For over 150 years, the "World's Largest Store" has remained a retail innovator with an impressive list of firsts: in 1862 Macy's introduced the first in-store Santa; in 1864 elaborate window displays gave birth to a new breed of buyer, the window shopper; and in 1866 Margaret Getchell, Macy's superintendent, made history as the first woman retail executive.

Rowland Hussey Macy, *Nantucket Whaling Captain, Merchant.* Started Macy's in 1858 at Sixth Avenue and 14th Street. The Macy's red star logo was based on a tattoo he got as a young Nantucket whaler.

Isidor and **Nathan Straus,** *Merchants.* Originally leasing the rights to the store's glass, china, and silver departments, they took controlling interest in Macy's after Rowland Macy's death in 1877, and in 1902 moved the store to its current location.

De Lemos & Cordes, *Architects.* Designed the original Broadway building.

Robert D. Kohn, *Architect.* Designed the Seventh Avenue addition.

Macy's department store actually consists of two buildings: the original Broadway building and the 1924 Seventh Avenue addition. The nine-story building (200 ft. w x 700 ft. l) is constructed of red brick and limestone. On the Broadway facade, the middle floors are articulated vertically with superimposed bay windows and four-story-high Corinthian pilasters. Above the bay windows are *Palladian*-style arched windows. The main selling floor has been restored to reveal the 1930s *Art Deco* style, and the store's original wooden escalators are still in use.

The four caryatids (columns shaped like women) on the 34th Street facade entrance (inset) are by J. Massey Rhind. Other original details on the 34th Street facade include the canopy, clock, and turn-of-the-century Macy's lettering. A plaque at the main entrance memorializes the 1912 death of Isidor Straus and his wife on the *Titanic*.

National Historic Landmark 1978.

Fred Gailey: *"Is it true that you're the owner of one of the biggest department stores in New York City?"*
Mr. R. H. Macy: *"THE biggest!"*

—From the Academy Award–winning film
Miracle on 34th Street (1947)

"*I think that New York is not the cultural center of America,
but the business and administrative center of American culture.*"

—SAUL BELLOW
Canadian-born American author

New York Stock Exchange

The big board

18 Broad Street

Completed in 1903, the current New York Stock Exchange building (the original, since demolished, stood at 10 Broad Street) houses one of the most important financial institutions in the world.

The **Buttonwood Agreement** (May 17, 1792) is the original document drafted by 24 brokers to form the *New York Stock Exchange Board*. It was named after the buttonwood (sycamore) tree under which their trading of bonds began. A buttonwood tree was planted outside the entrance at 20 Wall Street to commemorate the organization's origins.

George B. Post, *Architect.* Awarded commission for his design.

The *Greek Revival* building has a rusticated two-story base with rectangular and rounded arched openings. Six 52-foot-high Corinthian columns support a classic Greek pediment. Behind the columns, a four-story glass curtain wall admits light into the marble and gilded trading room, 109 x 140 ft. with 72-foot marble walls.

The statuary in the pediment, *Integrity Protecting the Works of Man,* designed by J. Q. A. Ward and Paul Bartlett, includes: *Integrity,* center, *Agriculture* and *Mining* on her left, and *Science, Industry,* and *Invention* on her right, representing the sources of American prosperity. The original marble statuary was destroyed by pollution and replaced in 1936 by copper and lead figures, coated to resemble stone.

The New York Stock Exchange Board has 1,366 members and more than 2,800 companies listed on the exchange. The price of a seat has fluctuated over time: in 1817, a seat cost $25; in 1929, $625,000; and ten years later, $85,000. In 2004, seat prices reached $4 million in anticipation of the end of seat sales, due to a merge that would make the NYSE a for-profit publicly traded company. In 2007 the NYSE Group took a global step by merging with Euronext, and in 2008 NYSE Euronext acquired the American Stock Exchange, adding more than 500 Amex-listed companies to the exchange. Tours of the trading floor have been suspended since 9/11.

National Historic Landmark 1978. N.Y.C. Landmark July 9, 1985.

THE MORGAN LIBRARY AND MUSEUM

Fit for a priceless collection

225 Madison Avenue at 36th Street

This elegant three-building complex houses the collection of **John Pierpont Morgan** (1837–1913), scion of the powerful financial empire. Well known for his gifts to education and the arts, Morgan spared no expense in constructing what has been described as "among [the] most luxuriously appointed private museums in the world."

McKim, Mead & White, *Architects.* The original 36th Street *Italian Renaissance*–style building, completed in 1906, was constructed of marble blocks laid up without mortar in the manner of classical antiquity. At this time, McKim, Mead & White were the pre-eminent East Coast architects, working in the eclectic classical style espoused by the *École des Beaux-Arts* of Paris, the world's foremost school of architecture.

J. P. Morgan Jr., *Financier and philanthropist.* Morgan's son and heir (1867–1943) opened the Library to the public in 1924 and dedicated it as a research institution. In 1928 he built the Annex to connect to the original McKim library. Under the terms of the gift, the Library will be kept intact until 2013, the 100th anniversary of his father's death.

Renzo Piano, *Architect.* Creator of the library's 2006 $106 million transformation, Piano connected the three existing historical buildings by constructing three new steel-and-glass-enclosed pavilions and a light-suffused central courtyard, as well as additional exhibit and public space, and a 280-seat concert hall.

A major 2010 restoration of the McKim building's interior included additional exhibition spaces, new lighting, the opening of the North Room to visitors, and restoration of period furniture and fixtures. The collection includes prints, rare books and medieval illuminated manuscripts, paintings, drawings, sculpture, music manuscripts, children's books, and Americana.

National Historic Landmark 1966. N.Y.C. Landmark May 17, 1966.
N.Y.C. Interior Landmark March 23, 1982.

"*The only credential New York City asked was the boldness
to dream. For those who did, it unlocked its gates and its treasures,
not caring who they were or where they came from.*"

—MOSS HART
American playwright and stage director

TIMES SQUARE

Crossroads of the world

42nd Street at Seventh Avenue
and Broadway

Times Square is a triangular area created by the intersection of Seventh Avenue and Broadway at 42nd Street. During the late 1800s, the area was the center for carriage shops and stables, and called Longacre Square after a similar area in London. In 1904, the square was renamed Times Square in honor of Adolph Ochs's Times Building, home of *The New York Times* daily newspaper. The first theater in the area, the Metropolitan Opera House at Broadway and 40th Street, opened in 1893, and the theater district was born.

"The Great White Way" is a term supposedly coined in 1901 by O. J. Gude, an ad man for Broadway's glittering electric signs and billboards. In the 1920s, when movie palaces became the rage, the flashing displays reached new heights. Elaborate signboards, including a cascading waterfall, giant cigarette smoke rings, and monstrous neon tumbling peanuts helped create the Times Square visual mystique. By the 1970s, most of the movie palaces had been replaced by glass skyscrapers, and between these office buildings, pornography found a home. Since 1993, the Times Square District has been renovated and rejuvenated to its original status as the city's premiere entertainment center. At the northern end of the square stands a statue of American showman George M. *"Give my regards to Broadway"* Cohan, by George Lober (inset).

The world's first moving electric sign was installed on the Times Building in 1928. The 5-foot-high, 360-foot-long ribbon of 14,800 electric lights displays a message that travels around the building. After several years of darkness, the "motograph" was restored and reilluminated in 1986. It displays up-to-the-minute news flashes from the daily *New York Newsday*.

Times Square's first New Year's Eve celebration took place on December 31, 1904. It has remained an annual festive tradition, complete with the famous dropping ball and half-a-million revelers.

Once a gridlock of vehicular mayhem, in 2009 Mayor Michael Bloomberg introduced the Greenlight Manhattan project, which reconfigured traffic patterns in Times Square to allow for permanent pedestrian plazas. The initiative has increased motor safety, reduced pollution, and encouraged a renewed multi-use enjoyment of the area.

PLAZA HOTEL

A grand hotel de luxe

Fifth Avenue and Central Park South
at 59th Street

T his magnificent landmark hotel opened on October 1, 1907. The 19-story, cast-iron *French Renaissance* building cost a total of $12.5 million to erect and featured 800 rooms, five marble staircases, and a two-story ballroom.

Henry J. Hardenbergh, *Architect.* Also designer of the Dakota Apartments.

The hotel's first guest was Alfred G. Vanderbilt, son of Cornelius Vanderbilt, and it has since been host to famous guests and to society's parties and balls, most notably Truman Capote's 1966 Black and White Ball. A portrait of the best known and most troublesome resident—six-year-old Eloise, created by author Kay Thompson—hangs in the lobby. The Plaza has been the quintessential New York hotel for numerous films including *The Great Gatsby, North by Northwest, Funny Girl, Cotton Club,* and *Home Alone 2: Lost in New York.*

Its grand vistas, north to Central Park and east to Grand Army Plaza, afford the hotel one of the most prestigious sites in the city. Its exterior, a designated New York City individual landmark since 1969, consists of a three-story marble base with a ten-story mid-section of white brick, capped by balustraded balconies, a massive cornice, and a five-story mansard slate roof with dormers, gables, and crest. Two corners are rounded to form towers. Flags flying from the Fifth Avenue facade represent the nations of important foreign guests and dignitaries.

Once owned by Donald Trump, the Plaza was sold in 2004 for $675 million. It closed in April 2005 to begin a $400 million renovation project. Reopened on March 1, 2008, the Plaza now offers 282 guest rooms, 152 condominium residences, and retail space. Eight of the hotel's interior rooms are designated interior landmarks: the Palm Court, the Grand Ballroom, the Terrace Room, the Edwardian Room, the Oak Room, the Oak Bar, the 59th Street Lobby, and the Fifth Avenue Lobby.

National Historic Landmark 1986. N.Y.C. Landmark December 9, 1969.
N.Y.C. Interior Landmark July 12, 2005.

"*The New York Public Library is more than brilliant, more, even, than major.*"

—TONI MORRISON
American author

NEW YORK PUBLIC LIBRARY

Reading between the lions

Fifth Avenue and West 42nd Street

This building is considered one of the finest examples of *Beaux-Arts*-style architecture in America. The library was the result of a merger between the Astor and Lenox Libraries and the Tilden Trust, and was constructed on the former Croton Aqueduct Distributing Reservoir. The library opened on May 24, 1911.

John M. Carrère and **Thomas Hastings,** *Architects.* Awarded the commission based upon their competition-winning design.

Dr. John Shaw Billings, *First Director of the Library.* Credited with conceiving the library's basic plan. The Main Reading Room (297 ft. x 78 ft.) was one of Billings's suggestions.

The symmetrical Fifth Avenue facade, constructed of Vermont white marble, sits at the top of a broad flight of steps with expansive terraces on both sides. Three arched bays flanked by paired Corinthian columns form the main entrance. The wings have two-story-high engaged Corinthian columns. Between the columns are arched windows with sculpted lion's mask keystones. A bay with pediments and sculpture completes each end of the building. The building is lavishly ornate, both inside and out, with sculpted lions, cherubs, and gargoyles. Its 88 miles of bookshelves house over 34 million books, manuscripts, maps, and prints; its combined lending collections (books, audio, CDs, DVDs) exceed 50 million items. It is considered one of the five great research libraries of the world. On average, more than 11,000 people enter the library daily.

The statues of *Beauty* and *Truth* (L-R of the entrance) are by Frederick MacMonnies. Paul Bartlett designed the 11-foot-high figures of (L-R) *History, Drama, Poetry, Religion,* and *Romance* on the frieze. The celebrated lions (inset) are by Edward Clark Potter. Their original names were *Lady Astor* and *Lord Lenox.* Mayor Fiorello La Guardia renamed them *Patience* and *Fortitude.*

National Historic Landmark 1965. N.Y.C. Landmark January 11, 1967.

WOOLWORTH BUILDING

Cathedral of commerce

233 Broadway at Barclay Street

The Woolworth Building opened on April 24, 1913, when President Wilson pressed a button in Washington, D.C., illuminating its 80,000 lights. Designed in the *Gothic Revival* style, it took three years to build, and the construction cost of $13.5 million was paid for in cash.

Frank Winfield Woolworth, *Merchant.* After his first five-cent store failed in Utica, N.Y., Woolworth opened a five-and-ten-cent store in Lancaster, Pa., in 1879. Within 32 years, he had established a chain of over 1,000 stores, and the F. W. Woolworth Company flourished for another six decades.

Cass Gilbert, *Architect.* Also designed the U.S. Custom House and U.S. Court House in New York, and the Supreme Court Building in Washington, D.C.

The 792-foot building consists of a copper-clad pyramidal tower rising from a 27-story base. It was the world's tallest skyscraper for 17 years, until the Bank of Manhattan was completed in 1930. Terra-cotta covers the structural steel skeleton from the fourth floor upward. The ornate *Gothic* detailing of cream terra-cotta includes flying buttresses, pinnacles, sculpted gargoyles, mythical beasts, and masks. The lobby's caricature reliefs of Frank Woolworth counting his nickels and dimes (inset) and Cass Gilbert studying a model of the Woolworth Building were designed by Thomas R. Johnston. In 1998, after 85 years as Woolworth's corporate headquarters, the building was sold for $155 million. Just a few blocks from the September 11, 2001, terrorist attacks, the Woolworth Building suffered no significant damage, but as a security measure, the ornate lobby, once a popular tourist attraction, was closed to the public.

National Historic Landmark 1966. N.Y.C. Landmark April 12, 1983.

"New York is a granite beehive, where people jostle and whir like
molecules in an overheated jar…"

—NIGEL GOSLIN
American author and art critic

GRAND CENTRAL TERMINAL

The noble gateway to New York

42nd Street and Park Avenue

Designed in the *Beaux-Arts* style, Grand Central Terminal, a multipurpose urban center, was opened to the public in 1913. It was financed by Cornelius Vanderbilt's New York Central Railroad at a cost of $80 million.

Reed & Stem, *Architects.* St. Paul, Minnesota. This competition-winning design team was responsible for the original solutions to the building's functional problems.

Warren & Wetmore, *Architects.* Responsible for the building's overall design and its *Beaux-Arts* detailing. They also designed the New York Yacht Club.

William J. Wilgus, *Engineer and Vice President of the New York Central Railroad.* Following the electrification of the trains, Wilgus was able to bury the train yards north of the terminal and utilize the street-level air rights for real estate development.

The terminal's steel frame construction is clad in Stony Creek granite and Bedford limestone. The 42nd Street facade has three grand arches, each framed with colossal Doric columns grouped in pairs. Above the central arch is a 13-foot clock, surrounded by the sculpture of *Mercury, Hercules,* and *Minerva* by Jules A. Coutan. Below it is the statue of shipping and railroad magnate Commodore Cornelius Vanderbilt, by Albert De Groot, 1869.

The main concourse (120 ft. w x 275 ft. l x 125 ft. h) is a thoroughfare for well over half a million passengers a day. Recently restored at a cost of almost $200 million, by **Beyer Blinder Belle,** *Architects,* the terminal was rededicated on October 1, 1998. The marble stonework was restored, chandeliers regilded, and the vaulted ceiling's extravagant astronomical mural by Paul Helleu returned to its original splendor. A staircase was added to the east end of the main concourse (inset) to match the elaborate west stairs, a double flight of marble steps designed after the grand staircase of the Paris Opera.

National Historic Landmark 1976. N.Y.C. Landmark August 2, 1967.

METROPOLITAN MUSEUM OF ART

The largest art museum in the Western Hemisphere

Fifth Avenue, 80th Street to 83rd Street

The Metropolitan Museum of Art houses one of the world's most comprehensive art collections, with more than 3 million works of ancient, medieval, classical, and modern art in more than 2 million square feet of exhibit space. From its *Gothic* origins to its more recent glass-walled additions, the museum reflects the major architectural styles of the last century. Recent additions include the new permanent gallery for the Arts of Korea, which opened in 1998, and an expanded Greek and Roman gallery opened in 2007.

Calvert Vaux and **Jacob Wrey Mould,** *Architects.* Designed the original *Gothic* building, 1874–80, which faced onto Central Park. The arcaded center portion of the west facade is the only visible remnant of the original building.

Richard Morris Hunt, *Architect.* The building's orientation to Fifth Avenue was established in 1895 when R. M. Hunt designed the Fifth Avenue *Beaux-Arts* pavilion and Grand Hall. **Richard Howland Hunt** became *Construction Architect* after his father's death. At the main entrance, three monumental arches are flanked by pairs of Corinthian columns, which support massive blocks of stone. The blocks were intended for sculptures, but monies were never available.

McKim, Mead & White, *Architects.* Designed the restrained *Classical* north and south wings on Fifth Avenue, 1911–13.

Roche, Dinkleloo & Associates, *Architects.* Designed the three glass-walled additions, 1975–82.

Two of the city's landmark buildings have been incorporated into the museum: the facade of the old Assay Office building from Wall Street, built in 1823, is part of the American Wing; and the pediment of the Madison Square Presbyterian Church, 1906, is part of the Museum Library facade.

National Historic Landmark 1986. N.Y.C. Landmark June 9, 1967.
N.Y.C. Interior Landmark November 15, 1977.

"…and yet it is true that I derive genuine pleasure from touching great works of art. As my fingertips trace line and curve, they discover the thought and emotion which the artist has portrayed."

—HELEN KELLER
American author, activist, and lecturer

CHRYSLER BUILDING

Dedicated to world commerce and industry

405 Lexington Avenue at 42nd Street

In 1930, the Chrysler Building became the world's tallest building when architect William Van Alen had the 185-foot spire (assembled secretly in the fire shaft) added to the 925-foot-tall building. The Chrysler Building thus surpassed the just-completed 927-foot-tall Bank of Manhattan (the bank was designed by Van Alen's former partner and rival, H. Craig Severance). Van Alen's record was short-lived, however, as the Empire State Building, at 1,454 feet, was completed only a few months later.

Walter P. Chrysler, *Automobile Industrialist.* Founder and president of the Chrysler Automobile Corporation.

William Van Alen, *Architect.*

Originally begun as an office project for senator-turned-developer William H. Reynolds, the downturn in the economy forced him to abandon the project, but Chrysler purchased the unfinished building and envisioned its completion as a monument to his own greatness. The building cost Chrysler $20 million (financed entirely by his personal fortune), and in 2008 a 90 percent stake was sold to Abu Dhabi Investment Council for $800 million.

The 77-story *Art Deco*–style building celebrates the automobile as well as the modern skyscraper. Constructed with white ceramic brick with stainless steel ornamentation, the Chrysler Building was one of the first to use stainless steel (almost 30,000 tons of it) as a building material. The fourth setback (26th floor) is adorned with white and gray brick automobile patterns and is capped at each corner with 10-foot-high winged radiator caps (inset). At the fifth setback, eight stainless steel eaglelike gargoyles perch over the edge, made to resemble Chrysler's automobile hood ornaments.

The angular lobby, restored in 1978, consists of multicolored marble and granite; a ceiling mural by Edward Trumball that depicts the Chrysler Building, transportation, and industry; and elevator doors and walls, decorated with stylized floral designs of exotic inlaid woods.

National Historic Landmark 1976. N.Y.C. Landmark September 12, 1978.

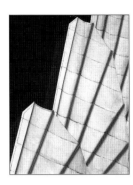

EMPIRE STATE BUILDING

The cathedral of the skies

350 Fifth Avenue at 34th Street

The Empire State Building was the world's tallest skyscraper from its completion on May 1, 1931, until 1973, when the former World Trade Center was constructed. Completed in just over 13 months, the Empire State Building cost $41 million to build, $19 million under budget.

Shreve, Lamb & Harmon, *Architects.*

John J. Raskob, *Developer.* Conceived of and raised the funding for the Empire State Building at a time when the country was in financial crisis.

Alfred E. Smith, *President of the Empire State Company.* Former Governor of New York State for four terms.

Built on the site of the original Waldorf-Astoria Hotel, the Empire State Building rises 1,454 feet to the top of its TV tower. Limestone, granite, nickel, aluminum, and more than 10 million bricks comprise the exterior. The building's basic components, windows, stone, and steel spandrels were fabricated off site and installed as if on an assembly line. The tower rises from a five-floor base and is capped with a monumental spire. The spire also acts as a lightning conductor and, as a result, the building is struck up to 500 times a year. The three-story-high lobby is finished in European marble, stainless steel, and glass that are arranged in geometric patterns typical of the *Art Deco* period.

Immortalized in the 1933 movie *King Kong,* the world-famous building withstood the impact of an off-course B-25 Bomber into the 79th floor in 1945. The top 30 floors were first illuminated in 1977, when the N.Y. Yankees won the World Series. Since then, the tower's colors change to mark various holidays and special events. Observatories on the 86th and 102nd floors offer unparalled panoramic views of the city, and are open to visitors daily.

National Historic Landmark 1986. N.Y.C. Landmark May 18, 1981.

"New York is to the nation what the white spire is to the village— the visible symbol of aspiration and faith, the white plume saying the way is up!"

—E. B. WHITE
American writer

ROCKEFELLER CENTER

A city within a city

Fifth to Sixth Avenues, between
West 48th Street and West 51st Street

Rockefeller Center was once the world's largest privately owned business and entertainment complex. Originally 14 buildings on 12 acres of land, it was the first development of skyscrapers designed as a group. Initially, the site was to provide a home for New York's Metropolitan Opera House. After the 1929 stock market crash, the Metropolitan Opera withdrew from the project, and in order to avoid financial disaster, the focus of the complex shifted to a mixed business center. The *Art Deco* complex, built between 1931 and 1939, replaced more than 200 smaller buildings in the area and employed more than 225,000 people during the Depression. In the 1960s and '70s, four additional towers along the Avenue of the Americas were added to the complex.

John D. Rockefeller Jr., *Developer.*

Hood, Godley & Fouilhoux; Corbett, Harrison & MacMurray; Reinhard & Hofmeister, *Architects.* These firms worked together to design the first architecturally coordinated complex in New York City.

The centerpiece of the complex is the GE Building (formerly the RCA Building). The slender limestone tower rises from a four-foot granite base to a height of 850 feet. The combination of high and low buildings with gardens and plazas creates the grandeur and spaciousness of Rockefeller Center.

More than 100 murals, mosaics, and sculptures, by 39 artists, adorn Rockefeller Center. Two of the best known sculptures are *Prometheus,* in the Sunken Garden, and *Atlas* (inset), in front of the International Building. The center is also home to Radio City Music Hall, NBC Studios, and the Top of the Rock™ observation deck on the 70th floor of the GE Building.

In 1989 the entire Rockefeller Center complex was purchased by a Mitsubishi subsidiary. Ten years later, Tishman Speyer Properties, L.P., purchased only the original *Art Deco* buildings from Mitsubishi.

National Historic Landmark 1987. N.Y.C. Landmark April 23, 1985.

RADIO CITY MUSIC HALL

Showplace of the nation

1260 Avenue of the Americas

When Radio City Music Hall opened as a vaudeville entertainment house on December 27, 1932, it was the nation's largest theater. The *Art Deco* styling combined with the palatial interior space celebrates a high point in American theater design.

Samuel L. "Roxy" Rothafel, *First Director of the Music Hall.* Famous for his combination of silent movies and live entertainment, Roxy was responsible for the hall's design and entertainment policies.

Donald Deskey, *Interior Designer.* Won the commission with his strikingly stylized *Art Deco* theater design.

The grand foyer (60 ft. H x 60 ft. W) is an entire city block long. It is graced with floor-to-ceiling mirrors and drapes, two 29-foot-long chandeliers, and a 24-carat gold-leaf ceiling. *The Fountain of Youth* mural by Ezra Winter is the backdrop for the foyer's grand staircase. The 5,933-seat auditorium is dominated by the golden proscenium arches radiating from the stage. Roxy's analogy was that of the sun setting on the ocean. The 144-foot-wide stage has a 43-foot-diameter turntable and three cross-sections that can be lowered or raised independently. The stage's hydraulic system was so innovative that the Navy studied it for its applications to aircraft carrier technology.

The world-renowned precision dancers *The Rockettes* moved to the music hall from the Roxy Theater in 1934. With a company of 60 dancers, 36 perform on stage at a given time.

Saved from demolition in the late 1970s, the hall continues to be a venue for premiere film showings, live stage productions, concerts, television events, the Moscow Circus, the Grammy Awards, and the famous annual Christmas Spectacular. In 1979, the music hall's interior was restored to its original 1930s design.

N.Y.C. Landmark April 23, 1985. N.Y.C. Interior Landmark March 28, 1978.

UNITED NATIONS

Promoting international peace and security

First Avenue, from 42nd Street to 48th Street

The United Nations complex of three buildings—Secretariat, General Assembly, and Conference Building—was designed by an international committee of 14 architects. Its 18-acre site was purchased with a gift of $8.5 million from John D. Rockefeller Jr. Built from 1947 to 1953, the cost of the three buildings was approximately $67 million.

Le Corbusier (Charles-Édouard Jeanneret), *Design Architect.* French (born in Switzerland). Credited with the conceptual design for the complex.

Wallace K. Harrison, Harrison & Abramovitz, *Architectural Chairman and Construction Architect.* Also the Director of the Board of Architects for Lincoln Center.

Trygve Halvdan Lie, *First Secretary General of the United Nations, 1946–53.*

The name "United Nations" was coined by President Franklin D. Roosevelt in 1941 to describe the countries allied against the Axis Powers in World War II. The name replaced the "League of Nations," which had been established by the peace treaties of World War I. In 1945, the UN Charter establishing the United Nations was drafted by its original 50 member countries. There are now 192 nations represented.

The Secretariat is the 39-story, 544-foot-tall vertical building. Completed in 1950, it was New York's first building with an all-glass curtain wall; green glass set in an aluminum grid rises unbroken to the roofline. Its north and south elevations, 72-feet wide, are covered in Vermont white marble. The General Assembly is the sculptured limestone building with concave roof and central dome. The Conference Building, facing the East River, links the Secretariat with the General Assembly. The Dag Hammerskjöld Library, opened in 1961, is linked to the Secretariat Building. The land occupied by the UN Headquarters is considered international territory, although it is subject to U.S. laws.

SOLOMON R. GUGGENHEIM MUSEUM

Let each man exercise the art he knows

1071 Fifth Avenue at 89th Street

The Guggenheim Museum is one of the city's most unique and controversial buildings. After 16 years of design and construction changes to accommodate the city's Department of Building Codes, the museum's directors, and public outcry, the museum opened in October 1959. The building's "organic" spiral form was completely foreign to the traditional uptown Fifth Avenue facade of aligned rectangular buildings facing Central Park.

Solomon R. Guggenheim, *Copper Magnate.* Established the Solomon R. Guggenheim Foundation for his collection of non-objective art.

Baroness Hilla Rebay, *First Director of the Museum.* Under her guidance, Guggenheim's collection shifted from the Old Masters to abstract art. She was instrumental in creating both the collection and the museum, and in commissioning Frank Lloyd Wright to design the building.

Frank Lloyd Wright, *Architect.* A paramount force in modern architecture and design. The Guggenheim is his only building in New York City.

Completion of the project was facilitated by the efforts of **Harry Guggenheim**, president of the foundation after Solomon R. Guggenheim's death in 1949, and **James J. Sweeney**, the museum's second director.

The museum is constructed of cream-colored reinforced concrete. The main gallery—an expanding spiral—is attached to the administration building—a smaller circular structure—by a concrete slab. An eight-story annex was completed in 1992. The art is displayed along a quarter-mile-long ramp that spirals 92 feet up to a domed skylight (inset). The permanent art collection housed in small galleries off the ramp includes works by Paul Klee, Wassily Kandinsky, Marc Chagall, Robert Delaunay, and Fernand Léger.

In 2008, the museum completed extensive restoration to the concrete facade, and interior improvements.

N.Y.C. Landmark August 14, 1990.

"*All day long I add up columns of figures and make everything balance. I come home. I sit down. I look at a Kandinsky and it's wonderful! It doesn't mean a damn thing!*"

—Solomon R. Guggenheim
American copper magnate

*"Lincoln Center may be Pagliacci to you but it's
Richard Rodgers to me."*

—RALPH G. MARTIN
American author

LINCOLN CENTER

For the performing arts

Columbus Avenue to Amsterdam Avenue,
62nd Street to 66th Street

Lincoln Center, a 16-acre complex of buildings that cost $185 million to construct in the 1960s, is dedicated to drama, music, and dance, and remains the largest, most comprehensive performing arts center in New York City. It caters to an annual audience of 5.5 million and supports a staff of more than 6,800.

Robert Moses, *New York City's Slum Clearance Administrator.* He proposed turning the area (formerly aging row houses) into a cultural venue.

John D. Rockefeller III, *Head of the Building Committee.*

Wallace K. Harrison, *Director of the Board of Architects.* Also a member of the architectural board for the United Nations and Rockefeller Center.

Surrounding an elevated plaza, the buildings are rectangular in plan, with flat roofs and colonnades, and finished in white travertine marble. Their *Classical* style and layout is often compared to that of an ancient acropolis. A major redevelopment and expansion project, meant to completely modernize and transform the complex for its 50th anniversary, continues at the time of this printing but is largely complete.

The three principal buildings are: The **Metropolitan Opera House,** 1966, **Wallace K. Harrison** of Harrison & Abramovitz, *Architect.* Facing Broadway at the center of the plaza, the Opera House dominates the complex. Behind its 10-story-high arched glass walls is a vista of plush red carpets, sweeping marble stairs, and a gold leaf ceiling. In the lobby are two large murals by Marc Chagall; The **David H. Koch Theater** (formerly the New York State Theater), 1964, **Philip C. Johnson** and **Richard Foster,** *Architects.* Located on the south side of the plaza, the David H. Koch Theater is the home of the New York City Opera and Ballet; and **Avery Fisher Hall,** 1962, **Max Abramovitz** of Harrison & Abramovitz, *Architect.* Housing the New York Philharmonic, Avery Fisher Hall stands on the north side. In an effort to improve the acoustics, the concert hall has been renovated several times. Other buildings in the complex include the **Vivian Beaumont Theater,** 1965; the **New York Public Library for the Performing Arts,** 1965; the **Juilliard School of Music,** 1968; and the **Guggenheim Band Shell,** 1969.

*"A hundred times have I thought
New York is a catastrophe, and fifty
times: It is a beautiful catastrophe."*

—LE CORBUSIER
French-born architect

This edition published by Universe Publishing by arrangement with DoveTail Books, dovetailbooks.com

Universe Publishing
A Division of Rizzoli International Publications, Inc.
300 Park Avenue South
New York, NY 10010
www.rizzoliusa.com

2011 2012 2013 2014 / 10 9 8 7 6 5 4 3 2 1

Printed in China

ISBN-13: 978-0-7893-2223-4

Library of Congress Catalog Control Number: 2010935639

Endpapers: *Map of the city of New York and island of Manhattan, as laid out by the commissioners appointed by the legislature, April 3, 1807, William Bridges, city surveyor; engraved by P. Maverick.*
Geography and Map Division, Library of Congress

For more information visit newyorklandmarks.com

Scale of One